I0756320

FINISHING LINE PRESS
www.finishinglinepress.com

Edge Habitat

poems by

Elizabeth Moore

Finishing Line Press
Georgetown, Kentucky

Edge Habitat

ISBN 979-8-89990-479-0 First Edition

ACKNOWLEDGMENTS

My gratitude to the editors of the following publications where some of these poems first appeared, some in earlier versions:

Boston Literary Magazine and Mass Poetry's *The Hard Work of Hope* series: "Corvid Spring"

Pangyrus: "Nor'easter (February, 2015)" (under original title "New England February"), "Love Song", "Chemical Pregnancy", "Edge Habitat"

Print Funeral: "The Bee in Groton Forest, in Memoriam"

Publisher: Leah Huete de Maines
Editor: Christen Kincaid
Cover Art: Elizabeth Moore
Author Photo: Kenneth Moore
Cover Design: Elizabeth Maines McCleavy

Order online: www.finishinglinepress.com
also available on amazon.com

Author inquiries and mail orders:
Finishing Line Press
PO Box 1626
Georgetown, Kentucky 40324
USA

Contents

To Nate, and to Sam and Arthur—my love and my hope

Love Song

> *"Like a swift migrating fish, the word cellulite has suddenly crossed the Atlantic."*
> —*Vogue, April 15, 1968*

Come, sea ripple. Come, ocean swell
of the world that seethes inside me—make me
shimmer like air on an open fire. I've been running
from you too long, my becoming body. My survival,
my second wind. My shoal schooling shoreward, persistently
pressing the rims of its own knowledge. How beautifully you insist
yourself on my ass—the love in my husband's cooking. And on my
stomach—
the belly laugh in my beer. And on my thighs—sweet riots of wild
raspberries. Come
swift as migrating fish with your wake of stretch marks, your currents
that curve somewhere—
render me the map of a long voyage, a route for retracing by hand.
Remind me I'm better than bone
reef, smarter than shipwreck. Shiver this storm-stilled skin—cast its
shade and shine in every direction.

Nor'easter

February, 2015

These are the months that test the hidden
frameworks of things: the studs within
the walls of home and body—both of which,
you suspect, are now becoming tenuous at best,
having already seen you through the previous
plagues of winter, and never creaked louder.

Even your faith suffers these days. You
hear "another blizzard" and find yourself
braving the miniature frozen world inside
the fridge again and again, ensuring that
you have enough milk, even though you know
you already checked it earlier this morning—
the knowledge of this perhaps also nagging
at you as you make your way back to the couch,
and sit there, and brood, and start to worry
instead that you might be experiencing OCD.

You look for ways to distract yourself from
these morbid thoughts. You tell yourself
it's only snow, after all—that another world
will surely come after this—and with
this new boldness to bolster you, you go
to your window, open the shade, and gaze
into the whirlwind that your front lawn has
inexplicably become, at the acts of creation
and dissolution happening there—a new earth
of frozen milk, it seems, over-layering the old.

"God, why?" you ask the whirlwind, and when
it hurls its white cloud of broken glass at you
(just like you knew it would), you do the only
thing you know how to do—the only thing
anyone can do in a New England February, when
the lintels of doorways all across the kingdom

are threatening to fail beneath the weight of
some dread angel's passing, its behemoth gray
shadow blotting out sun and color, its leviathan
shoulder nudging at the icy crust of the world.

You go back to your fridge, open the door,
and face that inner cold once again, re-ensuring
that you have enough milk—reassuring yourself,
too, that you will paint the studs of your bones
with it, that you will hunker down and wait out
this last rage of winter, this final breaker of king
and subject alike—that it, too, will soon pass over
you in favor of another, less fortunate first-born,
leaving you intact, your own lintel untouched.

The Bee in Groton Forest, in Memoriam

I wonder what it was like for you
to find yourself sitting in the
seat of my husband's jeans,
how it felt to be surrounded
by such wildness, such fibrous
cloth, and with what audacity,
what ancient know-how, you
stung him on the ass while he
dressed—while I gathered our
survival gear and shoved it into
the car, our tent with its insect
resistant sheath, as if we had
somehow finished with nature,
as if we could pack it away,
as if with our endless DEET
we could have prevented you:
your nerve in our human forest,
meeting one end with another.

Gray Foxes

For Nate, remembering Grape Island

For the inevitable extinction—
for the tide that rises between us,
muddying deadfall and driftwood
plank, barnacle shell and bottle cap,
seafoam and Styrofoam—for when
our own names elude us, this self-
same island, this glistering strand—
this slurry of sand grains and glitter
between the rain-gnarled woods
and the carnival lights of the city
where we squatted once, you and I,
with our fire between us, a pair
of Campbell's cans whistling in the
inferno—where, in spite of all we knew
we'd one day lose, we knew we were
also lucky when that skulk of unknown
animals started circling us in the dark,
each nameless, beloved, ephemeral—each
an instance of shadow and flame walking.

Carousel

For my father, remembering Casino Pier, NJ

Turning and turning again
at ocean's edge—returning
wave for wave and laugh
for laugh—I hugged my horse
and rode its rolling saddle
into your arms, each turn
returning you unchanged,
never lost, never losable—
I thought—to a sudden turn
of events, to storms of mind
and floods of body, horses
that we ride and can't turn.
What remains in a hurricane's
wake except sea and memory?
Your hair even then turned
gray—its wave above your brow
an Atlantic floodtide. Little
happens that hasn't happened—
your own parents gone by then,
unknown to me from a calliope
endlessly looping, though present
in every wave you returned
from the shore. So we turn
to this world, this sea song—love
insisting on something rather
than nothing. A carousel still
turning in my memory, turning
underwater, turning again.

Whimbrel

Kendall Square, Cambridge, MA

Wind-driven, wading through downdrafts,
I stumble over her corpse on the soaked sidewalk
and think about hope: a sea bird, all molt
and mottle, her curved bill tossed back in
the dinosaur way of her kind. She has just had
the wind knocked out of her. How else to account
for the spine's impossible arch—the beak and tail
lifting to touch in a unified curl? Overhead,
the reinforced windows of Google and Microsoft,
the brutalist walls of the Innovation Center. I don't
know the name of this animal, just as I can't
identify where this city begins or ends, where fill
transforms into flood. Weather turns over the estuary.
Roosting under an overhang, I tap *migrating birds*
near Boston into a search bar, and uncover in seconds
the name of the walloped wader: one from a flock
of thousands darting southward through squalls
and cyclones, mating on mudflats, and thriving
in shallow water. *One out of many,* I think, mourning
the broken bird with her ill-fated feathers. Then,
angling into the wind—*Out of many, one.*

Trying to Conceive

> *"Then Medb got her gush of blood...it dug three great channels, each big enough to take a household."*
> *—The Táin, translated by Thomas Kinsella*

How to go all in on the ordinary
when the ordinary is what we've been
wanting least? This morning my gush
of blood—I think of her in that cycle's
final moments, squatting in brambles,
brought low by her own body. If I could
carve channels with period blood, I would—
if I could create landforms, bring whole new
worlds into being with menses, I would.
Meanwhile how to live with these cramps
and clots—these common threads? What to do
with another month gone? I hunker over
the toilet, relieving myself—*spare me*,
I beg of this world with its sword of years,
knowing that in that story she gets to live,
that an answering swell might exist for each
canyon she carved. This is how we envision
horizon—a convergence of sky and soil,
a landscape-to-be. This is how we keep
trying again.

Corvid Spring

Bird-watching soars amid COVID-19 as Americans head outdoors
—AP headline, May 2, 2020

Since I cut your hair on the patio
the backyard birds have been threading
it into their nests. Now chicks come
of age in your curls. Early mornings
I hear them clamoring to be fed, all mouth
and inborn insistence cleaving the shell
of the cold. What to make of all this life
and all this sickness? How to account
for this world? Up the road, at the asphalt
refinery, I recently heard a man and crow
going at it, one cawing back at the other
in call and response, as if arguing or speaking
a common language. Crow to man, or
man to crow—you couldn't have said who
was who, who wanted to keep living more.
Nothing to do but make do; the nests hold
forth through the seasons. The inexorable
earth turns summerward as your hair
grows in to feather the tips of your ears.

Chemical Pregnancy

I still wonder what became of you,
almost child, assortment of elements—
if you linger somewhere, nothing lost
and nothing gained, an equation
only. The red line of you faded
to memory, released in blood—
the red tide of me flowing you
seaward, unbearing you forth.
Are you nowhere now, formless
flotsam, a nameless nothing? Or
are you living a thousand lives
with a thousand names—the matter
of you in each glistening fish scale
and foil scrap? Years before you,
I nearly failed chemistry—there were
too many kinds of bonds for my
mind to carry. I couldn't hold it,
it wouldn't stay in me, things went
awry—and perhaps in the end this is
all we ever are, this matter of us
in its ongoing making and breaking—
still, I remember you; somehow
this body, this matter, remembers:
how little we knew of you in your
almost rooting, and how knowing of
you was almost too much to bear.

Midden

In spite of everything, I can't bring
myself to hate it—the dumping ground
in the woods behind the house.

The lengths of decrepit pipe
and decaying bole, the gnarls
of vine and wire, of root and old rug.

I can't hate everything falling apart
and building up, everything becoming
everything else—soon I'll be turning

forty, never not already always
a changing body. I wade through
the burls and brown bottles,

the schist and slag, and think
about love as submission
and bend to this place—this rusty

file cabinet replete with dead leaves
and mystery. I have to believe
in the givenness of this life.

In the heart with its heavy metals,
the bones and bisphenols, the blood
composed of PFAs and plasma. Repair it

but first love it—love that we are
so deep in this given world, so up to
our throats in litter, we never leave it.

It doesn't reclaim us so much
as it welcomes us home.

Benediction for Sam

April, 2022

In the beginning, when
we couldn't hold you yet,
we held our own hope—
something we could still
nurture. It wasn't until later,
seeing you in the NICU
cradled by tubes, that we finally
caught our own breath: you
living, learning to breathe
on your own. What had you
known of this life except blood
and metal, felt except blade
and swaddle? Son, I will not lie
to you: in time you'll come to know
this world as a hospital, an edgeland
of living and dying threaded
with care. Go into it—breathe
deeply; love deeply. Know
that this is our hope for you.
Know that this is enough,
that this is everything.

What This Still Wants

To eat and be eaten, more than
anything else. To be both
starved and sated, eaten out.
To keep making milk months
later—to feed in each sense
of the word, to be constant
and conduit. To be whole in
its holes, to be holy, to hallow
its hollows—to meddle and
middle and muddle, embrace
its own water. To remember
the sea it came from and never
left—to be that sea smoothing
the stones of itself on its tongue.
To ask and ask and ask and ask
again what it is that it wants—
to move with its waves of desire,
its in-and-out tides. To touch
and be touched, to love and be
loved each time. To do what
it does and to be what it is
each time. To be here each
time. And each time. And
each time. And each time.

Going Gray

For Nate, in solidarity

Not a loss of color so much as becoming
contrast—a kind of shimmer. A thickness
of branch & vine on crown & temple
unframing our faces: the two of us here
in the midst of this—space & time. Or
something that was ourselves once, for who
can catch these slipping visages, hold
these bodies—your hands sloughing dust
just as much as my face in your palms?
I haven't lived long but I've lived long
enough to know this: we are both of us
constantly shifting & constantly shedding.
We are not who we were before, who we
will be tomorrow, so let's be these glinting
threads, this burgeoning silver—how it flares
in the sun, how it longs in the dark, how it is.
How it is & is again & again & again—
the insistence of this & the plenitude, one
after another—so that now, when I find strands
of hair on the bathroom floor, I can't say
if it came from the comb or our own hands,
if it's animal or human, yours or mine.

Berrypicking with Sam

He offers me half-bruised bundles
in purple-stained palms, imploring me—
babbling *ahhh* and *mm-mmm*
mm-mmm—to play my part, parting
my lips, and to swallow them down.
They coat my tongue, softened with
sunray and swollen with squall—
black raspberries growing wild,
sweet and sour. Above all I want
to warn him about the thorns—
see my two hands reaching out
before pulling back. Want to say,
Things can be hard. Want to tell
him I have known my share of
suffering. But he reaches in faster
than I can hope to stop him, already
leaning so deeply into this world,
angling into the weave at the edge
of the woods, that today if not
tomorrow I choose to believe it:
that this instinct, too, is my offspring,
runs strong in my line—that all of this
bramble is more than enough to feed
us, this matter constantly mattering,
living and dying, all ripening
here on the rims of things, over
and over—the fruit, and the thorns,
and the juice of it all running down.

Nor'easter

December, 2023

2023 has been the "year of the brink"...
—CNN headline

This is a squall like any other, only beginning
and only passing, save this: the basement floor
welling away from its moorings. The carpet
a mud-gray sea that ripples when touched—
shivers from furnace to freezer and back again—
the silts in your concrete foundation remembering
wetting. Save this: the strata of years that suddenly
surface—the pen-pricked notebooks, needle-stitched
blankets, and palette knife paintings. Save therapy
notes, save depression, save OCD. Save this but not
that: the books but not the bookshelves, the fabric
but not the Singer, the paints but not brushes. Hunker
down, batten and buckle, but mostly believe it: this
endless edging of everything forth—the frayed nerves
of the trees. Believe some things are still worth saving
though given to mold—that lightning from cloud
and clod meet somewhere halfway. Believe all that
is being shown here again and again—in everything
moving, in nothing not constantly flowing. Believe in it all
being well, in all things welling—in thunder, your own
open mouth. In wind bank, your own flexed muscle.
In cloudburst revealing the depth of your own longing.

Edge Habitat

"Come / home. Everything is begging you."
—Ada Limón, "It Begins With the Trees"

We come upon it rounding the edge
of Brook Hollow—the sign that marks
the verge along the path.

Storm-weathered, standing at angle,
worn fence post beside it, barbed wire
and bramble interlaced at its base.

And just beyond, through a scrim
of bittersweet, wind-blown pasture—
orderly lines and rows of new-mown grass.

Everything is happening here—
a respiration, an adaptation, a kind
of survival. *Edge habitat*, the sign

tells me, *is a transition zone*
between two adjacent habitats—
but where is this edge I've been

walking, this place of transition?
Where is the fence of the body,
the wall of the breath?

***

edge, noun.
The thin sharpened side of the blade
of a cutting instrument or weapon;
opposed to the 'back' or blunt side

edge, verb.
To harrow.

***

When my first was born, he almost
wasn't born. He was gray as another
planet—no heartbeat, no breath.

So I breathed for him as we watched
from the edge of the room—I sang beneath
my breath as they rubbed him down,

as their hands, so many, impressed
on his heart to keep beating, wanting him
here to that rhythm, wherever *here* is—

I sang, praying hard to this world
to hold him close, and though I like to think
my song was what brought him through,

it was their care, their genius
that carried him back from the brink—
it was others who bore him, this world

in the form of their hands,
when the boundary line of my body
refused to release him.

***

on edge
anxious, nervous

***

As a child I was terrified of edges—
of needle-points, blades in the eye.
I imagined that wounding as hard

as I possibly could—saw the prick
and pop of membrane, the streams
of ichor. I thought if I could see

it hard enough, see it through
in my mind to its logical conclusion,
I wouldn't actually see it

through with my own two hands.
This worked—I still have my eyes,
but my mind has its blindness:

it forgets how to see
there's a place between fear
and wonder.

***

edge, noun.
incisive or penetrating quality

***

And maybe none of this
is new so much as all of this
is always already new—

maybe no edges exist
when all this world is an edge,
when there is nothing

we can make of all this
except making it, nothing
we can see except what is

here. *The hardest thing of all*
to see is what is really there—
J.A. Baker with his peregrines,

like the one I've seen pricking
the power lines over the street
and now spiraling over the field

with a knife for a beak.
A knife, an edge, a scalpel
that opened me up—opened me

just enough to pull him through
into living and dying and living
and dying to live, into being here,

being an edge on this edge
of all things—into feeling
his being, insistent as a blade.

***

on edge
adjoining, close by

***

Edge habitats are more diverse
than adjacent habitats—this too
says the sign by the path

where I've been standing, all
nerve and hormone, all flight
and intrusive thought. Showing

already—my second child's heart
beating low in my belly. The orbs
of the eyes fully formed, the lungs

near finished—*Will he breathe?*
I have to worry. *Will he live?*
Consulting the sign again,

I read that *species requiring both*
open and forested areas utilize
edge habitat. Which will he be,

I wonder—field or forest or something
of both? No knowing, no telling,
but always this constant carrying—

always already here inside me,
already at home. The hardest thing
to see is what's really here.

***

edge, variant of *age*, noun.
The length of time (sometimes given
as a specified number of years)
that a living thing, as a person, animal,
plant, etc. has lived.

edge, noun.
a favorable margin

***

So here he is, and here I am,
and here we are—and I've been
trying so hard to be at home

in this world that I've forgotten
I'm already here at home
in this world, and maybe this

is a kind of home, a kind
of habitat—a breath flooding in
and out of a body littoral—for

if depression is stagnation, what
isn't this world? Who aren't we
but our own transitions, our mean

evolutions? Fear and wonder
and something between—the hardest
to see. Everywhere and nowhere

but mostly everywhere—these forests
and fields overlapping, these creek beds
of care. We are here for now

watching the peregrine riding
the thermals, until my son kicks
and I'm walking the path toward

home, my two eyes opening slowly
with fear and wonder—an animal
who has never been more human.

Notes

In “Edge Habitat”, definitions of “edge” and related phrases were lifted directly from Merriam Webster Dictionary and OED online.

“if depression is stagnation” is a modified line from Sandra Cisneros’ essay “The Beautiful Unforeseen”—“What is depression if not stagnation?”—published in *Orion*, Autumn 2022.

Elizabeth Moore is a poet and fiction writer. She is the author of The Truth and the Life (Alternative Book Press), and her poetry has appeared in *Pangyrus, Print Funeral, Boston Literary Magazine,* and Mass Poetry's *The Hard Work of Hope* series. Born and raised in southern New Jersey, she lives with her husband and two sons in Massachusetts.

www.ingramcontent.com/pod-product-compliance
Lightning Source LLC
LaVergne TN
LVHW090541110826
845146LV00003B/1216

* 9 7 9 8 8 9 9 9 0 4 7 9 0 *